This book is dedicated to my parents, William and Mary.
—P. H.

To my sons, Vicente and Joaquim
—R. A.

ATHENEUM BOOKS FOR YOUNG READERS • An imprint of Simon & Schuster Children's Publishing Division • 1230 Avenue of the Americas, New York, New York 10020 • Text © 2024 by Philip Hoelzel • Illustration © 2024 by Renato Alarcão • All rights reserved, including the right of reproduction in whole or in part in any form. • ATHENEUM BOOKS FOR YOUNG READERS is a registered trademark of Simon & Schuster, Inc. • Atheneum logo is a trademark of Simon & Schuster, Inc. • Simon & Schuster: Celebrating 100 Years of Publishing in 2024 • For information about special discounts for bulk purchases, please contact Simon & Schuster Special Sales at 1-866-506-1949 or business@simonandschuster.com. • The Simon & Schuster Speakers Bureau can bring authors to your live event. For more information or to book an event, contact the Simon & Schuster Speakers Bureau at 1-866-248-3049 or visit our website at www.simonspeakers.com. • The text for this book was set in Cormorant Garamond. • The illustrations for this book were rendered in watercolor and pencil on recycled paper. • Manufactured in China • 1023 SCP • First Edition • 10 9 8 7 6 5 4 3 2 1 • Library of Congress Cataloging-in-Publication Data • Names: Hoelzel, Philip, author. | Alarcão, Renato, illustrator. • Title: Planting hope : a portrait of photographer Sebastião Salgado / Philip Hoelzel ; illustrated by Renato Alarcão. • Description: First edition. | New York : Atheneum Books for Young Readers, 2024. | "Season: Spring 2024". | Includes bibliographical references. | Audience: Ages 4–8 | Audience: Grades 2–3 | Summary: "Sebastião adored exploring the paradise of his parents' farm in the Mata Atlântica forest of Brazil. From atop a hill, he would look at the world from a new perspective and dream of what might lie beyond his view. Then, when he went away to school, Sebastião met Lélia, who showed him how to use a camera for the very first time. When Sebastião looked through the camera, he realized he could use photography to organize how the world fit together. Because of his talent for seeing what others could not, Sebastião traveled the world and took pictures for all kinds of news stories. But after witnessing too many painful images of environmental destruction and violence, he put away his camera and returned with Lélia to his childhood home. But, when they arrived at the farm, the land was in ruins. So Lélia suggested they rebuild the rainforest and make their efforts an example to others. Through art and activism, Sebastião and Lélia would show that everyone was connected to a large ecosystem and responsible for its care, and that all may not be lost if we take action"— Provided by publisher. • Identifiers: LCCN 2020026198 | ISBN 9781534477650 (hardcover) | ISBN 9781534477667 (ebook) • Subjects: LCSH: Salgado, Sebastião, 1944—Juvenile literature. | Photographers—Brazil—Biography—Juvenile literature. • Classification: LCC TR140.S334 .H64 2021 | DDC 770.92 [B]—dc23 • LC record available at https://lccn.loc.gov/2020026198

Planting Hope: A Portrait of Photographer Sebastião Salgado
written by Philip Hoelzel   *illustrated by* Renato Alarcão

Atheneum Books for Young Readers
NEW YORK LONDON TORONTO SYDNEY NEW DELHI

In the town of Aimorés,
in the Mata Atlântica forest of Brazil, there lived a boy
named Sebastião. Like his seven sisters and thirty-five
other families, he worked on his parents' farm.

Once Sebastião finished
his chores, he adored
exploring his paradise. . . .

He swam with the
caimans and played
under a waterfall.

He trotted his horse
through the forest while
anteaters, tropical birds,
and ocelots peered at him
through the foliage.

He walked with his father to the
lookout on a hill, where he dreamed
of what might lie beyond his view.

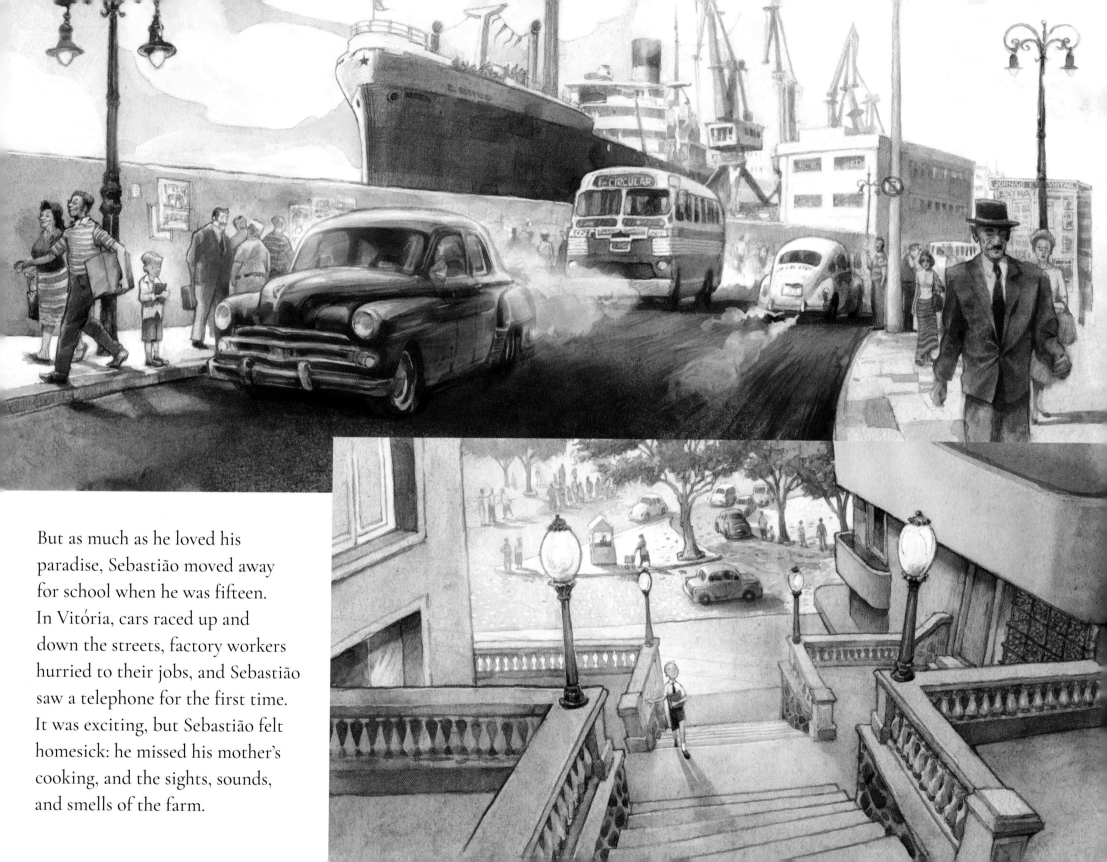

But as much as he loved his paradise, Sebastião moved away for school when he was fifteen. In Vitória, cars raced up and down the streets, factory workers hurried to their jobs, and Sebastião saw a telephone for the first time. It was exciting, but Sebastião felt homesick: he missed his mother's cooking, and the sights, sounds, and smells of the farm.

Then, years later, he met Lélia, a smart young woman who was finishing her studies. They fell in love, got married, and moved to São Paulo, Brazil. There, Sebastião studied economics to help people get the food, shelter, and money they needed to thrive. But the government was in turmoil, and life became dangerous for anyone who spoke out against it. So they fled to Paris, France, and continued their studies. Sebastião finished his economics education while Lélia studied architecture.

One day, Lélia purchased a camera to take pictures for a class. Sebastião picked it up. He turned it this way and that. He had never used a camera before. Then he looked through the lens. *Click!* Just like that, he took his first photograph.

When Sebastião looked through the camera, he realized he could use light to illuminate his subjects. It was the same light of his childhood that had pierced between puffy thunderheads or shined from behind his father as he approached Sebastião under a shaded tree. In this way, Sebastião could organize how the world fit together.

After graduation, Sebastião borrowed Lélia's camera and traveled to Rwanda, where he wrote reports about how tea farms provided people with work. He saw the farmers living in harmony with the land. Their connection reminded him of the people who worked on his beloved farm in Brazil, so he captured this relationship on film.

As he took pictures, Sebastião discovered something. . . .

Through the lens, he could show a story
he could not write in his reports.

Through the lens, he could share people's lives that might not be seen.

Through the lens, Sebastião could show how he saw the world.

Sebastião discovered he could influence more people by using pictures instead of written reports. Photography was a language that didn't need translation, and it showed how he felt. "Anything that hurts my heart or makes me happy, I want to see it and photograph it. Anything that I think is beautiful enough to show, I show it."

Because of his talent for seeing what others could not, Sebastião and Lélia left their comfortable life behind so he could become a photographer. He traveled the world and took pictures for all kinds of news stories.

Click! Beauty! Click! Presidents! Click! Wars! Soon, Sebastião's photographs were in demand, and he began to work for a humanitarian organization called Doctors Without Borders.

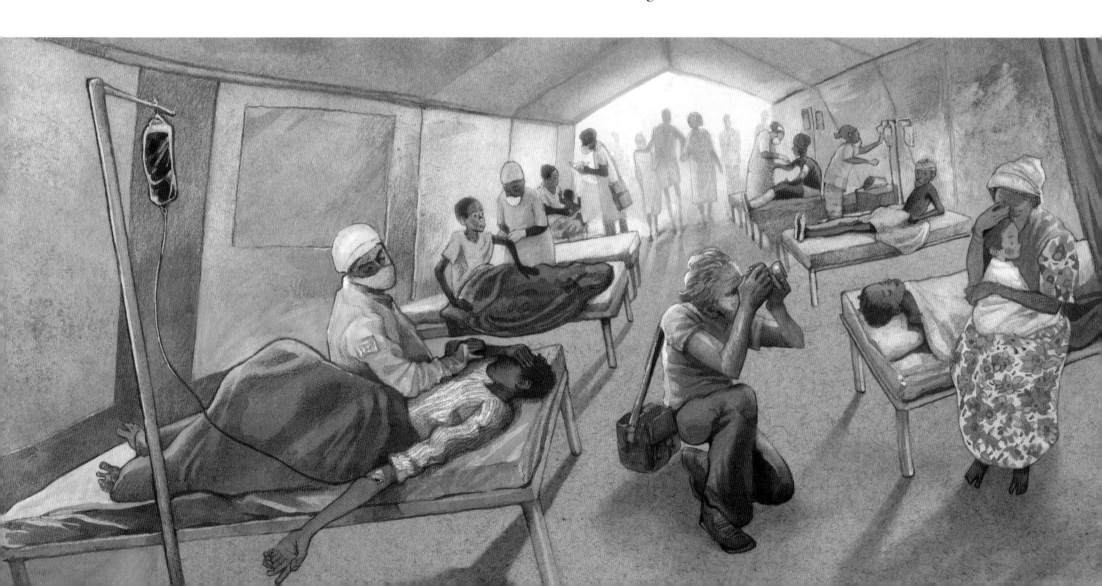

Sebastião also used his camera to tell stories about forgotten people. He photographed refugees leaving their homes because of environmental destruction and bigotry. He celebrated workers by showcasing their skills. He recorded people fighting in wars, as a warning to future generations. He used his talents to capture a world that was constantly transforming.

One day, Sebastião photographed a story that changed him. When he went back to Rwanda, he witnessed a civil war that killed thousands of people. Seeing so much death and violence made him sick. Sebastião felt hopeless—humans seemed like a cruel species with little willingness to change. So, once this project was complete, he put down his camera. He no longer wanted to share what he saw of this hurtful world.

With no desire to take photographs,
Sebastião and Lélia returned to Brazil.
Sebastião's family had given him
the farm of his childhood. Perhaps
returning to nature would heal him?

But when Sebastião and Lélia arrived at the farm, the land was in ruins.

Brazilwood, ironwood, and peroba trees that held water in the soil and provided shade on hot, sunny days had been cut down for lumber. The soft forest soils were wearing away. The ocelots, anteaters, and colorful birds were gone.

Lélia cried to see the sickness of the land.

Sebastião wept over the destruction of his childhood paradise.

Then Lélia thought of something that gave her hope. "Sebastião," she said, "you always told me that you grew up in a paradise. Let's rebuild your beautiful world. Let's plant the rainforest that was here before."

Sebastião had photographed people destroying their environment. Not just in Aimorés, but all over the world. Sebastião agreed with Lélia: they would make their efforts to save the forest an example to others.

But could it work?

Sebastião contacted a forestry expert who created a plan for planting more than two million native trees. In the hot sun and humid air of Aimorés, Lélia, Sebastião, and the workers moved slowly up the steep hills, cut and dug up the grass, and planted one hundred thousand trees.

But six months later, more than half of the trees had died. Sebastião and Lélia discovered that the holes they had dug for the seedlings were too small. Now they had to start all over. Yet they did not give up or lose hope.

Year after year, Sebastião and Lélia cared for their forest. They learned from their mistakes, and each time they planted, more trees survived.

As the trees grew and the land slowly healed, Sebastião healed too. He felt life coming back into him as he witnessed the return of the missing trees, birds, and animals.

Sebastião wanted to share the hope that he felt, and he knew just the way to do it. So he picked up his camera and, with Lélia, traveled the world with a new idea: to celebrate humanity's relationship with nature.

Sebastião focused his camera—and the world's attention—
on the last remaining natural places in order to save them.
For eight years, Sebastião photographed mountains and
oceans, forests and deserts, and rivers and icebergs. He told
a story about whales and caribous, penguins and bears, and
elephants and lions.

And he photographed Indigenous peoples in the Amazon rainforest to show how humans continue to live in harmony with the planet.

Sebastião realized that many people living in cities had forgotten they were a part of something bigger. He wanted his new photographs to remind people of where they came from. That they were connected to a large ecosystem and responsible for its care. Sebastião and Lélia wanted to show the world that all may not be lost if we take action.

And now . . .

In the town of Aimorés, in the Mata Atlântica forest of Brazil, Sebastião and Lélia have an environmental education center in the rainforest they rebuilt.

A place where ocelots roam and endangered macaws, woodpeckers, and parrots can nest.

A place where people respect and care for nature, and nature gives back by providing them with water and clean air.

A place where knowledge is shared, so children can plant and care for a forest of their own.

Author's Note

In 2015, my friend Carlos recommended I see a movie titled *The Salt of the Earth*. It was about a man named Sebastião Salgado. Sebastião's work as a photographer and humanitarian meant a lot to my friend. Once I saw the movie, I too had respect for Sebastião. So much so that when I traveled to Brazil, I made sure to stop by Sebastião's childhood home to see the piece of land that he and his wife, Lélia, had replanted. While there, I took a tour of the property. I visited the tree nursery housed on-site, saw where the seeds of the native trees were stored, and took a wonderful walk through Sebastião and Lélia's forest. I came away hopeful and inspired, and my wish is that this story has provided you with hope and inspiration too.

Thank You

My heartfelt thanks for helping bring this book to life goes out to Bethany, Donna, Phyllis, Gillian, my editor Julia, Miranda and my critique group (Candy, Chris, Greg, Julie Ann, Kristen, Lauren, Nancy N., Nancy M. B.), plus Sebastião and Lélia Wanick Salgado, the team at Instituto Terra, and many others.

Instituto Terra—The Environmental Education Center in Aimorés, Brazil

When Sebastião and Lélia Salgado created Instituto Terra, their first project was to replant about seven hundred soccer fields' worth of native trees on Sebastião's boyhood farm. To help grow enough trees to finish their project, they created a nursery to raise many of the 290 different species of trees they needed for their section of the Mata Atlântica, or Atlantic Forest. In order to make sure their seedlings were healthy, Sebastião and Lélia opened a science laboratory for biologists to study tree seeds and make their research findings available for free.

Today they have grown more than four million seedlings. Many of these seedlings have been used on projects that have helped save seventeen thousand acres of land (approximately eleven thousand soccer fields) in the Rio Doce river valley near Sebastião's boyhood home. These seedlings are part of Instituto Terra's efforts to bring approximately three hundred thousand springs back to life by working with local farmers to plant mini-forests. This project will take decades to complete.

Aside from growing seedlings and planting trees, Instituto Terra receives visits from local schoolchildren and trains young farmers. The schoolchildren learn about the history of the Rio Doce region and tour the tree nursery. The farmers live on the property of Instituto Terra and learn agricultural techniques designed to restore and preserve the Mata Atlântica.

The Mata Atlântica, or Atlantic Forest

Where Is the Mata Atlântica?
The Mata Atlântica is located in the countries of Brazil, Paraguay, and Argentina.

How Big Is the Mata Atlântica?
The Mata Atlântica stretches along the Brazilian coast from the state of Rio Grande do Norte in the northeast down to the state of Rio Grande do Sul in the south, and west into the countries of Paraguay and Argentina. Approximately 11 to 16 percent of the original forest is left in Brazil due to deforestation.

What Lives in the Mata Atlântica?
The Mata Atlântica is home to around twenty thousand species of plants and twenty-two hundred species of amphibians, mammals, reptiles, and birds. More than 52 percent of the tree species and 92 percent of the amphibians are endemic to the Mata Atlântica, meaning they are found nowhere else in the world.

Endangered species that live in the Mata Atlântica include jaguars, golden lion tamarins, woolly spider monkeys, maned three-toed sloths, and red-toed parrots.

A Partial List of Sebastião's Awards and Honors

German Book Trade Peace Prize (2019)

Foreign Honorary Membership of the American Academy of Arts
   and Letters (2019)

Member of the Académie des Beaux-Arts (2017)

American Sociological Association Excellence in the Reporting
   of Social Issues Award (2010)

Photographic Society of Japan International Award (2003)

Prince of Asturias Award (1998)

Royal Photographic Society Centenary Medal (1993)

International Center of Photography Infinity Award (1986,
   1988, 1994)

Hasselblad Award (1989)

World Press Photo Award (1984, 1992)

Select Photographic Essays Produced by Sebastião and Lélia Salgado

Amazônia (2021)

Genesis (2013)

Sahel: The End of the Road (2004)

The End of Polio: A Global Effort to End a Disease (2003)

Migrations (2000)

Workers (1993)

Other Americas (1986)

Please note that the artwork in this book is intended to represent Salgado's style of photography, rather than serve as a direct replication of specific works.

Bibliography and Other Sources

Bannister, Matthew. "Sebastião Salgado: My Love Letter to the Earth." BBC World Service, Outlook, April 11, 2013.

Cott, Jonathan. "Sebastião Salgado's Visionary Light." *Rolling Stone*, December 12, 1991.

Finkel, Jori. "Back to Nature, in Pictures and Action." *New York Times*, May 27, 2009.

Funk, McKenzie. "Sebastião Salgado Has Seen the Forest, Now He's Seeing the Trees." *Smithsonian Magazine*, October 2015.

Gracie, Carrie. "Sebastião Salgado, Photographer." BBC Sounds, 2010.

Huxley-Parlour. "Exclusive Intimate Interview with Sebastião Salgado at Beetles+Huxley, 2014." YouTube video, 54:15.

Instituto Terra. "Série Globo Rural." December 2011.

Leitão, Míriam. "Entrevista de Lélia Wanick e Sebastião Salgado." GloboNews, June 16, 2012.

Manzoor, Sarfraz. "Sebastião Salgado: A God's Eye View of the Planet—Interview." *The Telegraph*, April 12, 2013.

Neidl, Phoebe. "The Hidden World of the Amazon." *Rolling Stone*, July 16, 2018.

Salgado, Sebastião. *From My Land to the Planet*. Rome: Contrasto, 2014.

———. "In Pictures: Instituto Terra's Reforestation Project." *Forbes*, January 25, 2008.

———. "The Silent Drama of Photography." TED, February 2013.

Sempre Um Papo. "Sebastião Salgado e Lélia Wanick, Sesc Palladium/MG - Sempre um Papo 2015." Video posted March 26, 2015. YouTube video, 1:11:49.

Wenders, Wim, and Juliano Ribeiro Salgado. *The Salt of the Earth*. Decia Films and Amazonas Images, 2014.